Small Keys
Open Big Doors

Let's level up together!

By Curtis Paige

By reading this document, the reader agrees that under no circumstances is the author responsible for any losses, direct or indirect, incurred as a result of the use of the information contained within this document, including, but not limited to, errors, omissions, or inaccuracies.

About the Author

Curtis Paige is a youth support specialist improving the lives of at-risk teens through residential care. Although his career in helping change lives has been an important part of his life development, it is his everyday life experience that fuels his ambition. Another motivation Curtis had was one day being able to take care of his mother. Being the only child and growing up watching his mom struggle, Curtis knew he was going to take care of her one day. That was the plan until tragedy struck just one month after Curtis graduated from college with his degree in social work. His mother, Michelle, passed suddenly in her sleep. Moving forward, Curtis understands that he cannot allow anything to stop him from building a legacy his mom would be proud of.

Another inspiration is his two daughters, for whom he strives every day to set an example. As a single father co-parenting with their mother, Curtis understands the value of how he approaches life in determining the path that his children will follow.

He has written this book to be an inspiration to others just like himself, walking the road of daily life. He hopes to encourage his audience never to give up, follow their dreams, and take hold of their lives. Success is only as far or as difficult as a person perceives it to be. He hopes to motivate the reader to take ownership of where they are currently in life and become accountable for changing it for themselves and future generations.

Curtis is not an expert with many degrees or accolades. No! He walks the walk, talks the talk, and lives each day to the fullest. He has faced challenges, lost his mother, works hard to provide for his family, and has dreams and aspirations. He follows the steps he lays out in this book in his journey to success and looks forward to inspiring others to do the same.

Table of Contents

Introduction

Do you find yourself lost or in need of some guidance? Are you looking for answers and direction for your life? Well, you are not alone!

Life is hard, and we are constantly thrown curveballs, unexpected tragedies, distractions, and of course, opinions. We often have a vision of where we want to be in life but are unsure or question the process of getting there. For some, the very thought of taking a leap toward a goal or starting a project or business is terrifying and prevents us from taking any steps at all.

This easy-to-read guide is designed to reassure you that you are not alone and that you CAN take charge of your life, face the challenges head-on, and live out your dreams. Just because you may be going through something right now does not mean that these circumstances will be there forever, nor does it mean that you will never succeed. It simply means that you have to push forward toward your goal. Ultimately, the reward will far outweigh the struggle, and as you look back on where you came from, you will appreciate all that you learned along the way.

This book is about motivating you to take that next step, to begin your journey toward success, and helping you to stay inspired throughout the process. The road may not be easy, and you may stumble but rest assured that you will find within these pages the motivation to not only ignite the spark of innovation to begin but the tools that you need to continue down the road of this marathon of life.

Use the brief messages within this book as daily affirmations, inspirational dialogue, or the pep talk you need when your progress has stalled.

However you use it, be sure to meditate on each and breathe it in deeply. You will be amazed at the progress you can make toward your goals if you remain focused, disciplined, and have a positive mindset. Happy reading!

1. It gets greater later.

When striving towards a goal, you may not always see the results early on. The beginning may be rough, pose a threat or risk, and you may face obstacles. But, know that things will get better as time progresses. Life and your situation will not always be this way.

The results of hard work ALWAYS pay off in the future. Some day you will be able to look back and appreciate the effort that you put in to start a business, change careers, raise a family, etc. Although it may be difficult to see or understand while you are in it, hard times will pass. The situation will improve, your life will transform, and you will forget about the hard times as you enjoy the future.

As Abraham Lincoln is so famously quoted as saying, "This too shall pass!" Or, as I like to say, "It gets greater later."

2. It's only failure if you don't try.

You have to look at everything as a lesson. If you don't reach your goal after trying, putting in the effort, and attempting, then you have to look at it as a lesson. True failure is not trying at all.

Everything has or should have things that they want to achieve in life. Unfortunately, many people try to take a step toward their goal one time, and if it doesn't work, they quit. Taking that first step is often the hardest, but it does not mean that you have failed if that first step does not bring you closer to achieving your goal. All it means is that you are that much smarter and have learned something, helping you approach your goal differently or from a new space the next time.

The only way that you can truly fail is to quit altogether. In fact, nothing we do in life is a failure but rather just a lesson better preparing us for the next attempt.

When Thomas Edison was confronted about what some would call his "failed" inventions, he replied, "I have not failed. I just found 10,000 ways that won't work." Ultimately, Thomas Edison was responsible for 1,093 patented inventions.

Transform your thinking that the only way to fail is by quitting, and you will surely succeed at whatever you set your mind to. Failure is only for those who do not try.

3. Build your foundation on discipline.

Discipline is extremely valuable in accomplishing any goal in life. Discipline can be defined as using self-control or restraint. It requires self-regulation and consistency. For some, discipline means punishment or denying themselves things that they enjoy. However, it is the very act of denying yourself of those things that derail you from the task or steer your path off course that will help you succeed in life.

Discipline is the key ingredient in the formula to achieving anything in life. Runners do not wake up one morning and decide to run a marathon, participating in this grueling event without any training. They have set a goal of competing in a marathon and, therefore, must exercise discipline to keep them on the path toward their goal. This may mean implementing a schedule of distances to run, a number of days per week to train, and a regimented eating plan. It is easy to veer off the course and requires self-control and self-restraint to continue on the quest to achieve this goal.

Discipline is the foundation on which any goal is established, and without it, you can easily and quickly abandon your dreams, blaming other people or circumstances. In reality, the lack of self-control may have prevented you from achieving success. You can train and condition your mind through discipline to obtain whatever you want.

4. What are you willing to sacrifice?

Anything worth having requires some type of sacrifice. You may have to give up television, a certain food you love, or even hanging out with your friends. Unfortunately, these things are often just distractions, taking us away from our ultimate goal.

Depending on the path you choose in life or the goals you have set, you may be required to forego your guilty pleasures or something you enjoy to allow time and, frankly, energy to stay on the path.

The goal will determine the magnitude of the sacrifice. You would not have to sacrifice a dinner out with friends if your goal is to change careers. On the other hand, if your goal is to lose 15 pounds, a simple "no thank you" will have to suffice to remain on track.

Focusing on the goal will make the sacrifice more palatable, and ultimately, you will relish the fact that you have reached it. What you gave up will not appear to be as important or monumental.

To get what we want in life, we must eliminate those things that distract us from obtaining it.

5. Be the change you want to see in people.

The world cannot be better unless you change. We need to create the atmosphere we want to walk and live in. Change has to start with us.

As people, all members of the same human race, we do not value one another or our interactions. People are nasty to each other; customer service is not what it used to be; everyone has their own agenda and ulterior motive. There is no trust left in the world. If you want to see a change in the world, you have first to change what is inside you.

It has to start with the environment we create within the space we occupy in this big world. How do you speak to people? How do you treat others? How do you conduct yourself? Is your behavior worthy of being respected? Are you proud of how you present yourself to the world?

Change has to begin with you. Changing yourself and how you project yourself to others can cause a change in and how we interact with one another. You are not alone in wanting to see a change in this world. Why not be the change people want to see?

6. That's enough planning.

People often spend too much time thinking about the goal rather than acting on it. They mill over in their minds how they envision the outcome, what they want their lives to look like, and how they will enjoy achieving the goal. While planning is an important part of accomplishing anything in life, sometimes you have to just do it.

Once you figure out step one, you have to take the leap.

When you set your sights on something, you must create a plan and prepare for how you will get there. You would not leave home on a cross-country road trip without a plan. Of course, things will happen, roadblocks and detours, that will take you off course, and things will not always go as planned. But you cannot overthink the plan or the expected outcome and make progress toward the goal at the same time.

When a reporter asked Mike Tyson if he was worried about his upcoming fight with Evander Holyfield, he calmly replied, "Everyone has a plan until they get punched in the mouth."

Even the best-laid plans appear to be going well until something or someone comes along and knocks you in the mouth. What are you waiting for? The longer you contemplate your plans, the longer you delay your actions. However, once you get moving, things always fall into place.

It's time to get started. So stop overthinking and get out there and get moving.

7. If it were easy, everyone would do it.

Anything of value worth having in life is not easily attainable. You are going to have to work hard for the things you want. Maybe it is a sustainable income, improving your health, obtaining a degree, starting a business; none of these things are easy. Some goals require more effort than others; some may require you to make a sacrifice or change your behavior.

Whatever you set your mind to, know that it will not be easy because everyone would do it if it were. Everyone would become an entrepreneur if it were as simple as saying, "I want to own my own business." Millions of people would start and stick to a weight-loss journey if it was as easy as having the desire to be thin and healthy.

We should all expect to experience some difficulty in our lives. Nothing was meant to be handed to us or made available simply because we don't want to stress and struggle. You have to brace yourself for the challenges that will come but know that the reward will far outweigh the difficulties.

8. If you don't, then who will?

Everyone is capable of greatness; everyone is special in their own unique way. But only about 1% of people are willing to go above and beyond the rest, to get moving, push through, overcome, and succeed. This is not to say that the other 99% of people aren't great, but they don't go after their desires and dreams like the one-percenters who are hungry, eager, and willing to sacrifice to get what they want.

If it were easy, everyone would be a professional football player, have a best-seller, be on the big screen, or walk the runway. No! It is not easy, and no one will do it for you!

As the first-century scholar Hillel stated and is often quoted, "If not you, then who? If not now, then when?" Another question I would pose is, "why NOT you?" You are fully capable and have the same desires and goals as others. What is preventing you from taking charge of your life and moving forward?

Consider this statement again, "If you don't, then who will?" There is no better person positioned with your unique skills, attributes, and qualifications—why not join the elite group of one-percenters?

9. Be better than yesterday.

We all tend to lose a grip on life once in a while. Once we make a mistake or veer off course, our life continues the downward spiral, believing that there is no end until finally, out of control, we once again decide to make a change.

However, once poor decision or mistake does not have to be the start of something terrible or the end of something good. Every day that you lay your head down is the end of a chapter, the conclusion to the day. When you wake up the next morning, it is a clean slate, a fresh start, a new beginning to make new opportunities.

Just because yesterday was a wash does not dictate what today will bring. So what you didn't go to the gym yesterday, which is part of your plan and goal! Does it really matter that you didn't work on your business plan? Everyone stumbles or makes a mistake, but it does not HAVE to be the end of the road or the detour that stops your progress.

Today is a new day to work on making new opportunities for yourself. It is a new chance to make things better in your life or take that next step toward your goals. Set yesterday aside. What are you going to do today to be better than yesterday?

10. Rough seas create great sailors.

Embrace the hardship. The struggle will make you stronger. Sometimes people expect the easy path or very little struggle on the journey to reaching their goals. But, if you have never been tested, how do you know how good you really are?

Call it "battle-tested." If you train for a year for a marathon and then never enter the race, how do you know if you could complete the course? What if you never step out and try out that business idea? How do you know if it will be successful or not? A sailor can navigate the seas for years and never have to face the storm. Does the ease of calm waters demonstrate his prowess and skill as a sailor?

Facing your struggles and overcoming them makes you stronger, more knowledgeable, and better prepared for the challenges you will undoubtedly face later.

Don't let the hardship force you to quit. Embrace it, fight through it, know that there is a WIN in the struggle. Storms don't last forever!

Words of Inspiration

"Be thankful for what you have; you'll end up having more. If you concentrate on what you don't have, you will never, ever have enough."
~ Oprah Winfrey

"The two most important days in your life are the day you are born and the day you find out why." ~ Mark Twain

"There is always light. If only we're brave enough to see it. If only we're brave enough to be it." ~ Amanda Gorman

"I decided I can't pay a person to rewind time, so I may as well get over it." ~ Serena Williams

"Life is not so much what you accomplish as what you overcome." ~ Robin Roberts

“No one is you and that is your superpower.”
~ Unknown

“The best time for new beginnings is now.” ~
Unknown

“Every day may not be good, but there is
something good in every day.” ~ Unknown

“It does not matter how slowly you go as long
as you do not stop.” ~ Confucius

“Believe you can and you’re halfway there.” ~
Theodore Roosevelt

“Dare to know! Have the courage to use your
own intelligence.” ~ Immanuel Kant

“He who is not courageous enough to take
risks will accomplish nothing in life.” ~
Muhammad Ali

"Life is not a problem to be solved but a reality to be experienced." ~ Soren Kierkegaard

"The time is always right to do what is right." ~ Martin Luther King, Jr.

"'Life is short' really means 'do something.'" ~ Chimamanda Ngozi Adichie

"The happiness of your life depends on the quality of your thoughts." ~ Marcus Aurelius

"It always seems impossible until it's done." ~ Nelson Mandela

"There is no such thing as failure. Failure is just life trying to move us in another direction." ~ Oprah Winfrey

"To hell with circumstances; I create opportunities." ~ Bruce Lee

"Growth is the only evidence of life." ~ John Henry Newman

"Even if it makes others uncomfortable, I will love who I am." ~ Janelle Monae

11. Be patient, not content!

Being patient means that you're doing what you can, but you're not rushing the process, while being content means that you are okay where you are.

Jumping the gun and rushing the process can often work against you when working toward a goal. You have to be patient while continuously pushing forward. There is a fine line between being patient and allowing opportunities to flow, and many people jump ahead, not allowing the process to work for them.

Being content can also be equated with lacking ambition. And if you are stuck, content with where you are today, you may lack the ambition and desire to want and do more for yourself. Are you content? Do you move through life every day the same as the last? Or have you simply settled for what life has brought you?

There are always opportunities to be better. Are you willing to stay stuck, or do you have the ambition to be better? Often people do not want to be patient and are therefore willing to go to great lengths to circumvent the process and work hard. You may be unhappy with your financial situation. What are you willing to do? Cut corners selling drugs to get what you want? Or put in another application and wait patiently for the opportunity?

As legendary martial artist Bruce Lee said, "Patience is not passive, it is concentrated strength." While you do not want to be content with where you are, being patient will create opportunities.

12. You're the author of your own book.

As you go through life, you are creating your own story with every action, each decision, and of course, every mistake. You are the author of your own book – what story do you want to tell?

What you do with this one life you have is not dependent on anyone else. You are in control of the goals you reach, the accomplishments you achieve, and the struggles you face.

Know that you are not alone in your struggles, and there is not a person on the planet who does not face challenges of some kind. But, leaving a legacy of your life's stories all depends on what you want those stories to be about. How do you want your children and children's children to talk about you? Do you want them to speak fondly of you and your accomplishments with pride? How would you want to be remembered if you were to pass away tomorrow? What will people say about you? Will they say that you worked hard and achieved your life's dreams? That is what you should think about as you lay out the plans for your life and set your goals.

What is the story YOU want them to tell?

13. Acceptance.

On your journey for a better life, you know who you are. Accept the things you cannot change and do not allow them to hold you back or hinder your progress.

Understand where you are today compared to where you want to be. Accept the distance between your current position and success but do not be dismayed if the distance is great.

If you want to become a doctor and the number of years to reach your goal seems like an insurmountable mountain, accept the fact that everyone must start somewhere. Know where you are! If you have one hundred pounds to lose to reach your optimal weight, know that the pounds did not take a day to accumulate and will not take a day to lose. But you have to start somewhere.

In knowing your starting point, you will begin the process of moving forward on the journey.

Most importantly, accept the fact that you will not be in this position forever!

14. Trust the timing.

There is a process in everything. Nothing in life comes easily, nor docs it happen instantaneously. Life and, more importantly, success is a process. But, often, we find ourselves so eager to achieve the goals we have laid out that we become impatient and give up.

Have you ever wanted something so badly and eventually given up when it didn't happen in YOUR timing? Why? Why did you give up hope or abandon your dream? Have you considered that maybe the timing wasn't right? Maybe you were not in a position mentally or emotionally to be able to handle the success, the pressure, or even the stress?

Part of the process is accepting that what you want will come when the timing is right. It will come when you are ready. Sometimes your time is not the right time.

Accepting this fact requires nothing more than having patience. Understanding that you may not get everything you want when you want doesn't mean that it is ok to give up.

Patience is required for leveling up. Getting to the next level in life or one step closer to your goal requires time. Opportunities require time to develop; you need time to grow and mature. If you do achieve success before you have put in the effort to grow, learn, and develop, the success will be fleeting, and you will not appreciate it.

Think of the lottery winner who is suddenly thrust into the limelight of fame and fortune. While the financial freedom and abundance may be what they were striving for, the sudden onslaught of "family members" seeking assistance and making financial decisions can be overwhelming. They did not have to struggle and work hard to achieve this goal and did not have to face the bumps and bruises along the way that frequently provided an attitude of gratitude and mental fortitude. They often lose everything because the timing wasn't right for their success.

Trust the timing!

15. Don't expect to receive what you give out.

You cannot expect family members, co-workers, or even strangers to reciprocate your positivity, ideas, or goals. Expecting others to be on the same page will only set you up for disappointment and rejection.

Not everyone can see or appreciate your vision. Even those with the best intentions may try to deter you from reaching your goals. Do not take their low-frequency energy for life or dreams as your own. Their path is not your path, and each of us is on this life journey independently.

We don't all have or exude the same level of energy, nor should we have the same expectations of others. Just because you are a good friend, giving your co-worker a ride to work every day does not mean that they will be there for you when your car breaks down.

While seeing their point of view and understanding others' goals and desires is important, do not expect to receive what you give out.

16. Process then move on.

No matter your background, upbringing, education, or success, we all have one thing in common: we all live and die, and life goes on! We all experience difficult times, hardships, loss, grief, tragedy, and trauma, but we must go on.

It is ok to process your emotions about a situation or person, to grieve and mourn, but then we have to move on. Often people wallow in the struggle, keeping them stuck in the moment. It doesn't change the fact that the situation happened or the person is gone. Take the time you need to process all of it, whether days or months, but then move on. Moving on doesn't mean you value the person any less or the emotions of the situation are diminished. It simply means that life goes on.

Do not allow the trauma of the past to hinder your future. By holding onto those unresolved emotions or situations, you will be doing a disservice to those who depend on you for their success. You do not have to forget, but life does go on, so keep moving forward!

17. Take victories in the little things.

Have you heard the phrase "eat the elephant one bite at a time"? Like the goal or dream, the elephant seems to be a mammoth, an impossible task looming in the corner. For many people, the sheer volume of effort required to tackle it is enough to deter them from even starting.

But it is the small steps that matter. Every bite you take, each step toward your goal is a small victory and should be celebrated as such. The destination may seem too far to reach, but what if you set smaller, more attainable goals? Why not set the goal of losing 25 pounds and celebrate your accomplishment on your way to your ultimate goal of losing 100? You put a lot of effort and sacrifice into losing those first pounds, and while it may seem like one small step, it is still worthy of appreciation.

Every step moving you toward your goal is a positive one. You don't even have to see the whole picture, or as Martin Luther King Jr famously stated, "You don't have to see the whole staircase, just take the first step."

Celebrate the small steps along the journey.

18. Train for marathons, not sprints.

Life is like a marathon, a long-distance run of sorts. However, many of us train for speed, putting in place quick fixes with fast money. What did you learn along the way? Did you take time to appreciate the mistakes, heal from the disappointments, and stretch your muscles? Strength is developed over time when muscles are broken down and then heal. The struggles of life stretch our emotions, push the boundaries as far as they will go, and test our willingness to stick it out for the long haul.

Temporary solutions or "quick fixes" may cause more damage than help. Do you want to have a pocket full of money today but lack the resources and knowledge to sustain financial independence in the future? Are you willing to take on a temporary role or hop from job to job to fulfill an immediate need while jeopardizing your career path success? These "temporary" solutions only serve to distract you and your energy from the ultimate goal.

Always keep in the back of your mind, am I running a sprint, or will this help me in the marathon of life? Carefully consider new tasks or opportunities to identify if they will help you in the sprint or the marathon. How will it help me achieve my long-term goals? Be strategic in your decision-making, and do not hesitate to discard opportunities that will not benefit you on your journey to success.

19. Every day is a new chapter.

Every day is a new opportunity to create the best version of yourself. Every day you get to write a new chapter in your book. Every day you can make a new impression, build a new relationship, learn something new, forge a new path.

Creating the best version of yourself is a lifelong journey, and every day counts. Yet every day is a gift, and there is no promise that you will have another. There is no guarantee that the same opportunities will be presented to you tomorrow or in the days that follow. So, take advantage of every day and every moment to gain as much knowledge as possible, make the greatest impact, and become the best version of yourself.

No matter your goals or desires, there is no time like today to get started and make something happen. Or, as Benjamin Franklin said, "don't put off until tomorrow what you can do today," because tomorrow is not guaranteed.

Start your new chapter today!

20. What is success to you?

Success is in the eye of the beholder. Being successful can be seen differently by different people and even at different times in your own life. In your twenties, what you wanted and worked for may not be as important in your sixties. You may have reached your goal of acquiring your master's degree to find yourself in an entirely different industry later. Are you any less successful?

Maybe you define success as having a bank full of money, while someone else believes success is defined by the number of people they impact. Some may see success simply as waking up in the morning. Success is one of the most controversial topics because, in reality, how we each define success depends on our perspective, upbringing, and background. Your life shapes your perspective, and your perspective influences your life.

No two people will have the same perspective on life and, therefore, will not have the same goals and desires. But no matter what success looks like to you, it should equate to your happiness. Happiness should be the ultimate goal of whatever it is you enjoy. It should be the 'why' behind your motivation and the drive that gets you out of bed each morning.

No one can tell you what makes you happy, nor should they influence how you define success. Of course, you will have the nay-sayers and the "Debbie downers" telling you that you cannot do this or that, trying to discourage you from making moves. These people often do not have the willpower, discipline, or motivation to do what you are doing or are striving for. They don't want you to succeed because it will highlight their flaws and deficiencies. You don't have to stop loving them or push them away, but they should not derail your aspirations.

To help you determine what it is that makes you happy and how you define success, let's do a little exercise: The Three-Step Process

1) Describe what you want to be, how you see
   yourself being successful, or what you want to
   look like being successful.

____

____

____

____

____

____

____

____

____

____

look like being successful.___________________________

2) Where are you now?

3) What do you need to do to make yourself look like
what you have envisioned?

48

How will <u>you</u> be the author of your own story?

Conclusion

Thank you very much for reaching the end of the book. Hopefully, you will continue to use it as a tool or reference when the going gets tough or you need a little inspiration to take your life, your business, your finances to the next level.

The question is, really, how will you use the advice and guidance provided? Will this book become just another dust collector on your bookshelf, or will you refer back to it frequently to help maintain your momentum, fuel your passion, and reignite your spark?

No matter how you envision success or your dreams, you have to start somewhere. Even though that first step is always the hardest, it is also the most important. Apply what you have learned to push you one step closer to reaching your goals. When it seems like you are not making any progress or have taken a step backward, refer back to this guide to ignite the spark again to help you stay on the path to success. Remember that life is not about how quickly you reach the goal but rather what you learn along the way, the barriers you break, and the milestones you accomplish in the marathon of life.

9 798986 064949